WITCH TYRANTS

KAREN KELLOCK PH.D.

Manual for
Superior Men

A complete theory based on Einstein physics,
Political Psychology, Systems Theory
and Archetypal Psychiatry.

FORMULA
All success attraction
All disease obstruction
All recovery elimination

You must fast on all three
OBSTRUCTIONS:
People
Habit
Food

WITCH TYRANTS

She went from temporary stardom back to the original system and wow: what a shock in comparison. She rattled their cage with envy before, all that stored bad energy will now target her for sure. She got where any involvement was too complex: she just wanted to get home and fast. I'm telling you people aren't that important. People-worship is idolatry--profitless and pointless. Being so immature the kids get angry so fast the parents just cave into the vulgar and crass.

WITCH
TYRANTS

KAREN
KELLOCK

ESCAPING THE MATRIX

ESCAPING THE MATRIX

WHEN THE SCAPEGOAT LEAVES

Scapegoats are targets for blameshifting, shaming and displacing unresolved issues by aggressing.

The scapegoat is chronically mocked, punished and shamed for the shortcomings of Jane.

It also covers the relationship crimes that are committed by other family members, aye.

The abuse a scapegoat endures often leaves them emotionally challenged for life, tortured.

Toxic shame and intense feelings of loneliness make it hard to cut the cord despite the abuse.

The family cannot love them back in any enduring or consistent way so in utter sadness they stay.

The prospect of going it alone in the world disconnected from the tribe is terrifying, aye.

He doesn't care about you, it's all about him. Get that through your head and stop fantasizin'.

CELEBRATE ESCAPING THIS MATRIX

Now that you see who he is, be glad you escaped him. You've got your own thing from now on.

The heart is torn in two whenever trying to follow God and someone who's running from God.

Don't be a loudmouth, feminists are a turnoff. With men be silent: unless asked shut your mouth.

She attached a deep heart longing to a trivial relationship incapable of fulfilling her see.

You are loving correctly but using that love on the wrong person. He can't appreciate you/be gone.

It's fight, flight or FAWN: extreme people pleasing with the goal of not being hurt again see.

There is so much stress stored in the body and the psyche when adapting to this treachery.

His backhanded compliments and back stabs leave you in emotional confusion and sadness.

To tell if he's narcissist just criticize him lightly and you'll see a thin-skinned coyote start whining.

Narcissists take everything as personal attack so get ready: when not looking he'll get you back.

They're hostile, aggressive and angry with a murdering spirit. You can feel it yet you still go near it.

TRIGGERING SURVIVAL INSTINCTS

It triggers deepest survival instincts/abandonment fears like the orphan archetype, a destroyer.

To the wounded child separation feels like epic losses and the grief feels endless, though it never was.

To the tortured scapegoat the grief is endless BECAUSE it never was, that's the irony being stuck.

You're all alone in the world while knowing they don't like you and don't care if you're dead too.

Narcissistic abusers use scapegoats as dumping grounds for unresolved negative emotions.

Scapegoats grapple with feelings of inadequacy and low self-worth due to the system coming first.

After a lifetime of abuse/misjudgment the scapegoat cannot clearly see himself past or current.

With two older sisters in collusion with an alcoholic mother I was that down-putter to the gutter.

They made me miserable with their endless mean misjudgments and accusations. telling ALL.

Tho' I still have a chip on my shoulder, life in the country and healthy partners keeps me centered.

The triad couldn't regulate their own emotions or deal with stresses so dumped on me the bitches.

PREDICTABLE SUBSTANCE ABUSE

Developing substance abuse issues is a given. I smoked, snorted and drank for my healin'.

It was the only means of self-medicating the constant pain I carried, a hole in my gut from treachery.

They would spread stories that all believed. No judge or jury, I was never seen as innocent but guilty.

Sure I maladapted--but what came first? I lived in an emotional grenade range and needed solace.

The crap spread to the extended family I never met or any new relationships, always trashed.

I was in a grasshopper position 'til I met my husband who relocated me to an endless vacation.

It was a homesick feeling in my gut, a sense of being lost. Drugs & alcohol gave me instant solace.

I used food as entertainment, I was always happy when eating and that was a sick predicament.

I conquered these feelings when I started fasting at fifty. I made gold, after that I needed nothing.

My conversion from prior templates/systems was immediate. Water under bridge/it doesn't exist.

WHAT CAME FIRST? THE SYSTEM OF COURSE

What came first, the system or addictions to cope? They all drank, I was falling in/knew the ropes.

My grasshopper status attracted low men. In addition to my pain here was a whole new problem.

The pattern went on for decades and I was only saved, healed and sequestered through marriage.

People are really cruel to someone who's marked. "They love to hate" said a survivor of this war.

Untreated PTSD from being a scapegoat is common and that brings more abuse all around.

Unlovable, unworthy and fundamentally flawed: that's the self-image of an empath seen as odd.

It taught me to distrust my own thoughts, feelings and emotions. I was just a ghost waiting for heaven.

A scapegoat ignores his own needs, lowering his self-esteem. Then he can't relate to others or a team.

A three-against-one syndrome is like Cinderella and the prince represents a brand new life for ya'.

After being in that vise grip I enjoy every moment as a free lady and hip, a refugee from lunatics.

I wasn't permitted to speak--no 1st amendment rights. All is forgiven: now I speak day and night.

To lose your blessed sovereignty and have lesser people over thee is hellish and unAmerican see.

NOW YOU SEE WHO HE IS

The narcissist has kept you in a perpetual state of high alert and it's the body that breaks down first.

The constant activation of the stress response is draining. Jealousy triggers are a major thing.

Physical symptoms include panic, shaking and sweating, all part of a fight-flight scene.

Physical symptoms are a manifestation of the intense psychological stress living with narcissism.

Fight flight: you wanna fight but instantly hold back: [flight] in fear of his bad reactions, aye.

The push-pull of fight-flight creates things like shaking, anxiety attacks and never seeing the facts.

EMPATHS

Empaths are wired differently so it's important sweetie to know about yourself and set boundaries.

Empathic codependent people are magnets to low empathy narcissists. Get a boundary/grip.

People have become violent, even women are pugnacious. No conflict resolution skills I guess.

Get a country life if you can, it's the greatest glory still left on earth. The rest is globalism: dirt.

Untreated codependent empaths are set up to draw sickos--as we may predict--like magnets.

Toxic people are low empathy people. Low empathy means toxic. Get that thru your head sis.

#1: Empaths take on the energy around them. I went insane before learning to not let men in.

Their big hearts give too much despite receiving little. A system then takes over, drained and belittled.

Most can't handle the empath's complexity, depth and powerful capacity for love--so protect yourself.

Empath are so sensitive they may take on other's emotions as their own--and their demons.

Insecure people can't handle empaths so we need to be bullet proof at all times: hold your head up high.

An empath can't hold anything back even knowing it'll cost him the entire relationship, yah.

Hard to believe, but once healed that stuff doesn't stick anymore. You rise above: ridicule hits the floor.

We may have dimmed our light to appease insecure people but it's a balancing act with evil.

Empaths ask too many questions, they're into the details of life. The others hate that, aye.

People don't wanna break down the hard questions in life so it can lead to a breakup and strife.

HEALING

Once a victim sees there is a name for what they've been going thru, everything changes too.

Once the victim sees, she can never unsee. There's just something about the exact communality.

SEEING the common thread thru many relationships is a game changer for the victim: the end.

Once a victim learns definitions of the abuse tactic they've been subjected to, it's over Sue.

The narc attacks your problems by pointing out those having it much worse, but go within first.

PAIN OF LOVING SOMEONE

In the interim watch all the narc videos you can: when he hoovers again you're armed against this man.

An unequally yoked relationship will always hurt since it pulls the heart in two directions [cursed].

The pain coming from loving someone is a most important lesson and it came from God so listen.

The awful pain points to a part of your heart God wants to heal, like an early trauma or a raw deal.

Silence is golden because it's perfect. It fits every crevice and every unpredictable neurotic.

You're in alert mode 24/7 and your body is not able to rest. When that happens, illness or death.

If he's an insufferable narcissist he'll only make you unconscious so don't tell me you can't resist.

WITCH TYRANTS

TRAINED BY THEIR ANGER
APPEARANCE AND OUR DOINGS
VIRTUE SIGNALING NARCISSISTS
VANITY: FRUITLESS/POINTLESS/USELESS
NEGLECT IS CENTRAL
CONTROLLERS ARE BOUNDARY BUSTERS
WOMEN: MIRROR THE MAN
THE FALLEN HERO SYNDROME
INAPPROPRIATE GIFT-GIVING
NEVER YELL BACK, LEAVE
APATHY MIRRORS ORIGINAL TREACHERY
DEALING WITH NEGATIVE PROJECTIONS
FIGHTING SLANDER WITHOUT A SELF
MADDENING MISJUDGMENT
NEVER AGAIN, LEARN YOUR LESSON
FALSE ACCUSATIONS ALL AROUND
MARRIAGE SAVED THE QUEEN
ACTING LIKE THEY OWNED ME
WOMEN ALWAYS ON THE HORN
DUNNING-KRUGER EFFECT
JEZEBEL SPIRIT PREPARATION
LITTLE MINDS
HEINOUS HIPPIES
THE SLUT IS CROOKED
YOUR ENEMY BELIEVED EM
OBSTACLES ARE TRAINERS
GENERATIONAL ENVY
LET IT SINK IN: YOU NEED PROTECTION
THE SPIRIT OF FAMILIARITY
THE FALLEN PEOPLE/CHURCH
THE EVERCHANGING NARCISSIST
CHILDISH SILENT TREATMENT
EMPTINESS AND HOMESICKNESS
A MAN FINDS A WIFE NOT REVERSED
IMPERATIVE THINKING OF PRE-ADOLESCENTS
NEEDY FEMALES
LIVING IN GANGLAND HYPNOSIS
HE'S THE HIGH PRIZE NOT YO

WITCH TYRANTS

THE HERO'S PATH IS ZIGZAG
MY DETRACTORS/DEBATORS
NARCISSISTIC OUTSOURCING
UGLIFICATION FROM SIN
HE'S NOTHING WITHOUT EM
FAKERY BRINGS ASYMMETRY
YOU KNOW HIM BY NAME-DROPPING
LEARN WHO YOU ARE
THE NARCISSISTIC INFLUENCE
HUMAN FOIBLES DESCRIBED
HIS HIGH CONTROL NEEDS
SHE GOSSIPS CONSTANTLY
DUMB WITCHES
RULED BY FICKLE FEMINISTS
PEOPLE ARE CRUEL
YOU DON'T NEED THIS
BREAKDOWN FROM PATTERNS
SYSTEMS MAINTAIN HOMEOSTASIS
FAMILY RELIGIONS ARE FALSE
POETS HIT HARDEST
HE HAS NO INNER CORE
DOMINANCE NEEDS RESTRICTS HIM
DOMINANCE INHIBITS CONTENTMENT
TO RELATE, LEARN OF YOURSELF
DIVIDED LOYALTIES
HE DOESN'T GIVE A DAM, GET THAT MA'AM.
YOU HAD TO LEARN WHAT PEOPLE ARE LIKE
OVERCOMING NARCISSISM EVERYWHERE
BLOCK ALL CONNECTIONS
MEANINGLESS DETAILS
CURIOSITY KILLED THE CAT
DEVALUATION HURTS LIKE HELL
HE KEEPS A NARC HAREM
HE'LL INVENTS THE WRONG PLAN
SIN: SWIMMING IN MUDDY WATERS
SUDDENLY
THE DARK CLOUD OF FEMINISM
FURIOUS FEMINISTS

WITCH TYRANTS

BAN HER FRIENDS FROM THE HOUSE
MAKING PRE-CONVICTS
THEY CAN'T STAND IT WHEN WE'RE HAPPY
BE MINDFUL TO BANISH PAST THOUGHTS
THE END IS ALL THAT MATTERS
LIBERALS HATE OBVIOUS TRUTH
THEY IMPOSED ON ME CONSTANTLY
MILLENNIALS ARE SOCIAL CONFORMISTS
ATTACHMENT TRAUMAS
OPEN BORDERS IS OPEN VALUES
LIBERALS ARE GLOBALISTS
ERA OF DEGRADATION: HOLINESS IS SEPARATION
INVASION THROUGH NEPOTISM AND PERSECUTION
REVERSE RACISM IS REAL
THE WHITE PRIVILEGE SCAM
WALLS ARE NO SYMBOL OF OPPRESSION
ITS DUE TO IMMORALITY, NOT RACISM
CHRISTIANS CAN'T CONFORM
WITHOUT GOD'S SPIRIT IT'S MAD MAX FROM HELL
LIVING IN A GHOSTTOWN AND GETTING STRONG
BORDERS AND BOUNDARIES MEANS PARADISE
NEW LEVEL NEW DEVIL: OPPORTUNITY MEANS ADVERSARIES
DOUBLE FOR YOUR TROUBLE
THE NEW GOLDEN AGE IS UPON US
THROW EM OUT BEFORE THEY KILL YOUR DOG
OUR FUTURE HAS NO ROOM FOR OUR PAST
EVERY MORNING'S A BRAND NEW START
CLUTTER AND NOT-QUITE-CLEAN
FIND THE KEY AND IT'S ECSTASY
FASTING IS KEY TO BLISS
REVERSAL DIETING AND INTERMITTENT FASTING [IF]
AUTOIMMUNE AFTERTHOUGHTS
THE BACON BAROMETER OR LITMUS TEST
DON'T TOLERATE BULLIES
BE THAT CONSTANT SPOUT
STATE YOUR FAITH IN SUCCESS
CAN'T FORCE SUCCESS, PREPARE & WAIT
YOUR TIME HAS COME

WITCH TYRANTS

I got where any involvement was too complex. Just wanted to get back to the pad and fast.

I'm telling you people aren't that important. People-worship is idolatry--profitless and pointless.

If happily married and living, marriage is the answer to all ills because you're in perfect harmony.

Trauma: I never went into such a dark space. I saw hell on that day but ever since I'm all ok.

People go thru periods of physical illness and mental. Insanity: amazing I got away with it all.

The stress level was so high from the cluster of events I just lost it, a lunatic yelling for help.

I now see that people like me--need high walls--can get over-reactive and that's trouble see.

TRAINED BY THEIR ANGER

Being that immature they get angry so fast the parents just cave into the vulgar and crass.

They assume its bestiality cuz you love your dog. It's in THEIR dirty minds the filthy liberals.

I put up with your misjudgments for years but now I'm in victory dear and I aim to stay here.

Just cuz he comes to the door doesn't mean you gotta let him in but then I'm old fashioned.

WITCH TYRANTS

It doesn't look right to have a man in your home. Go out to dinner or instead be chaperoned.

It's unreal you'd let a man in your house not caring what neighbors think or conger up!

Ethology: studying animal-in-environment. Human ethology: mental illness is adaptive.

It's impossible to train them to respect me. The minute I set limits they busted my boundaries.

The fact he's lucid sometimes makes it worse cuz you never know what you're getting/cursed.

Instead of ruminating over past sins concentrate on talents and what makes you Karen.

Concentrate on your creative spirit coming thru on a daily basis cuz you've got routine patina.

You had to go thru a lot [yin-yang] to get here but now God removes the stain of those years.

APPEARANCE AND OUR DOINGS

He can't help how he looks, it reflects what he's doing. Until he repents he vacillates, boring.

It's sad common sense is seen as refreshing. It's like a light going off in the head suddenly.

A conservative is a liberal mugged by reality. Yah that's what happened to me see.

Not only will He take out slanderers but anyone who listened and believed em about yours.

There's something called etiquette and you don't have it. For one thing you impose or forget it.

WITCH TYRANTS

The vanity narcissist expects special treatment: best seat in the house and seen as distinct.

He draws attention to his achievements with easy ways to slip it into his conversations.

He's like: I've done a whole lot, I'm a somebody, I went on expensive vacations, I'm the king.

I know very important people: name drop. Get to know me better you'll be impressed non-stop.

On and on about all the important people he knows. Name drop is a red flag to hell below.

They are drawn to superficial signs of success. Showboat, best clothes, glittering friends.

VIRTUE SIGNALING NARCISSISTS

Virtue signaling: They make sure people notice when doing altruistic things like humble giving.

A generous chap: "make sure that's in our next newsletter"/"can you get a picture of that?"

His decent acts don't match his overall persona and that is much of the relationship trauma.

Vanity aglow: He's special clothes evincing an appearance of something but it's all show.

He's strongly offended when feeling slighted. Don't recognize him? You're unenlightened.

You don't recognize him as the high and lofty person he thinks he is? Then you're not legit.

They are never satisfied or content with what they have and it's never enough, get that?

WITCH TYRANTS

He is oblivious to other's reactions to his haughtiness and he can't see it when he regresses.

He's terrified of his own inadequacies to be exposed. Never talk about that, that's all you know.

He can't receive direction or advice. "Don't you know who I am?" He's mad this isn't realized.

Dip into past and you avoid growth. Avoid memory anchors to your grasshopper status of old.

He says "why would I need to listen to you? This is ME talking/don't you know who I am fool?"

Any questioning at all and he throws up his defense of grey rock, silence, grudges, strong walls.

VANITY: FRUITLESS/POINTLESS/USELESS

Vanity is conceit but it's also fruitless, pointless and useless: a going nowhere way of life sis.

Since he'll do anything for admiration he'll shift loyalties when it suits against you son.

Since he's a name dropper he's a social shifter and will switch sides when it benefits him sister.

He'll take bribes against his own wife. He has no loyalty only expediency in a phony life.

It's going nowhere, it has no purpose other than self-endorsement to get jollies for a moment.

He has no foundation. He states intentions but they don't happen & he's hopin' you're nappin'

A narcissist shows vanity in a pointless way of life needing constant admiration as supply.

Health: being content in simplicity & sufficiency; restraint in relationships in true humility.

Health: having gratitude, being modest and disciplined, going about one's work in quiet devotion.

Teachable, flexible, empathetic, caring: sound like your charming narcissist darling?

Realize these words are the opposite to the traits he's caught up in and he'll never change.

Dignity, respect, civility: filter your life thru these to avoid harsh egotistical pride penalties.

There's a pattern of NEGLECT in narcissists. Interestingly, the coverts are the most neglectful.

The covert is so into self he can't stand vulnerability so quietly slanders/sabotages you honey.

NEGLECT IS CENTRAL

Either way--covert or overt--the narcissist is neglectful and this characteristic is CENTRAL.

Signs of control needs: the message of self-centered superiority is "I don't care what you think".

If you don't admire him you're out of the club of Admirers for the Wisdom he puts out.

Your needs and feelings don't even register. Your corrections too tho' they cause anger.

Stop being imprisoned by the bums who drop in using you as a pit stop. Live formally/move up.

Your needs and feelings don't register with him. Get that through your dispensable noggin.

Being on the receiving end of this is so debilitating and insulting it sets you back to napping.

If you talk to him about making adjustments it's the "doesn't matter" reaction/failed again.

The bigger and more powerful the goal the more you must shut out like time wasters of old.

He throws me crumbs and I'm in heaven but then he's gone in a minute, that's the narcissist.

CONTROLLERS ARE BOUNDARY BUSTERS

You'll experience blurry boundaries around all controllers. They are boundary-busters.

The narcissist's conscience is flexible and fluid. Supply needs overrides morals as he knew it.

His manipulation of you takes precedence over conscience--the underdeveloped one.

The need for superiority overrides common decency, cooperation and compromise at times.

Narcissistic needs [for supply] overrides conscience in the narcissist and this is seen in conflicts.

In conflict they just lay all those morals aside pursuing control, superiority, lack of empathy.

Supply needs take priority over moral compass: that's pretty bad about the narcissist.

WOMEN: MIRROR THE MAN

Reverse your thinking. From "I need a man" to "I'm so glad I haven't settled for just anyone".

Mirror the man: give him what he gives you and nothing more. Stop chasing/have allure.

If he doesn't call you, don't call him. If he doesn't text you, don't text him. That's mirroring.

Computers make it easy for women to chase men looking innocent but it's all the same.

It should never be that women are the ones reaching out. Men are hunters and you are not.

You may reciprocate contact once he makes it but until then do your own thing and ignore him.

It wasn't him who broke my heart it was the attachment trauma bond with mom he triggered.

When I met you I learned the wisdom of elders: most people are only encumbrance/messers.

You need to exorcise: CUT THEM OUT. And everyone who knows them, flying monkeys or not.

When I cut her out and everyone she knew God breathed new life into me, whew!

You need to expurgate, bowdlerize: cut out the offensive/inappropriate blocking your rise.

She came bringing her friend, wearing me down. Then I bowdlerized and became renowned.

I hated em but mal-adapted thru denial until those moments final when I escaped the vile.

THE FALLEN HERO SYNDROME

THE FALL: First it was how to handle addiction then how to handle all the ramifications.

WITCH TYRANTS

The ramifications of addiction went out in concentric circles, ever-increasing into exhaustion.

The addict becomes a grasshopper in their eyes and then his trials really begin: DESPISED.

INAPPROPRIATE GIFT-GIVING

Because women are lovers they may love a man who is undeserving with little reciprocation.

If he texts interruptively in front of you then you do that too and he'll understand himself new.

Rather than being spoiled by your kindness in servitude he's become disrespectful and rude.

You can't just slather affection and adoration on an idiot who's using you like a dam fool.

He's a human conditioned by his past so your little gratuities make you seem needy/crass.

Your services and gifts will **NOT** make him a nicer person, get that through your head vixen.

NEVER YELL BACK, LEAVE

When he yells or threatens violence to mirror him would be to walk away/take no chances.

You don't yell back or curse back. You **REMOVE** yourself immediately and never look back.

You sidestep the power struggle as you've disarmed him and he learns not to do that again.

Never compromise self-worth/respect. If he sleeps with another woman you leave, that's it.

WITCH TYRANTS

If you yell like a fishwife back at him you're no better than him and he SEES that woman.

Yell back and you're just as worthless, lost, useless and reckless as he is. Get some class lass.

Sidestep the power struggle and move on. Now he sees what he deserves, facing his actions.

Insight: I'm a grown boy, an immature man. Since she won't accept that I need to man up then.

It comes down to one simple thing: never give a man more than he's giving you. Tony Gaskin

The man is the head so if he's outa line then YOU'RE outa line for serving him, get it?

APATHY MIRRORS ORIGINAL TREACHERY

Though he neglected her constantly she still wanted nurturance from him like a looney.

If you expect nurturance from him he says "no, I just don't do that, it is not in my nature".

The neglectful narcissist is disinterested in your humanity: what makes you you honey.

The apathetic narcissist mirrors the original trauma of rejection cuz they couldn't care less.

He doesn't care to know you, it's all about him. You feel it in your bones/reminds you of home.

Any requests for adjustments and its "you're so sensitive" or "you don't have it that bad".

Any requests are met with "all you do is complain, you're so negative, you just hate me".

WITCH TYRANTS

"I'm not interested in what you think would make things a little bit better" he said as he entered.

His lack of interest to know you deeply sis is the biggest sign of neglect & disrespect.

They don't do [make relationship better cuza my presence in it] kinda stuff, that's just tough.

We're not in competition in our own stream. It's not like if I get more you get less. It's infinite.

The problem is unresolved shame that puts the network in control: that's the game.

The hedge was down so I could see what I should want. In came evil so I wanted only love.

Just like the hedge is down for America so we see what we should want. It's Trump not chumps.

Your problem is taking it on. Just repent and forgive yourself if you did something wrong.

DEALING WITH NEGATIVE PROJECTIONS

I left off one association after another and escaped all evil talk. William James on the saints.

People don't know you and project onto you so if you don't stand up you'll be broken in two.

It was hard to deal with negative projections of others who didn't even know me--bummer.

If someone is empty/has no identity he's a sponge to bad projections until he knows "me".

If they haven't learned to deal with their own negative emotions they'll project em onto you son.

WITCH TYRANTS

All relationships are projections which allow us to see what's going on inside.
Jenna Ryan

FIGHTING SLANDER WITHOUT A SELF

Without a self, when confronted with false projections we internalize it as true and ACT IT OUT.

Swallowing [introjecting] negative projections brings compensations to deny the accusations.

Negative projections are horrible but a simple boundary can prevent any more trouble.

All will take advantage. Even the sweetest will gain power if you allow a boundary to relax.

MADDENING MISJUDGMENT

They came at me accusatorially and it was like they owned me. I felt possessed and lonely.

If I reacted [stunned] with anger it proved them right. How we react is crucial at this point.

I would try to disprove them, throwing me outa grace. In reacting to them I wasn't the Ace.

I'd try to be like Jesus who did not defend Himself. This was a hard life, an emotional hell.

Get outa there, go grey rock, go back to people who love you and who are human, amen.

There is no greater loneliness than to be so misjudged without being self-aware enough.

I internalized their negative projections for decades and acted out their evil narratives.

NEVER AGAIN, LEARN YOUR LESSON

WITCH TYRANTS

All you know is you never see that person again unchaperoned--protected from below.

I felt hopeless [stamped & bloodied by their projections] since it came from being dumb.

Even if I could explain myself they wouldn't have understood it--I cried out for God's help.

It felt like the witchcraft trials but it came from liberals! They were the worst accusers of all.

I ran to the arms of men for protection. It was a natural reaction for survival but things worsened.

FALSE ACCUSATIONS ALL AROUND

Men usually came around but it was the women I needed most protection from, dumbed.

I was weakened physically from their mean projections. I was failing fast from being harassed.

I got a Ph.D. to compensate, they accused me of lying about that and I believed them: fact.

Marry someone who loves and understands you and just talk to them. That was my solution.

MARRIAGE SAVED THE QUEEN

Everything--EVERYTHING--changed with a husband to protect me. The feminists are crazy.

By the time success finally arrives the female genius is so exhausted she can't enjoy it, aye.

Being alone is freedom, being with others is always having to explain myself to the dumb.

WITCH TYRANTS

Anger is a feeling which alerts you when boundaries are violated. Don't stuff it, heed it.

Anger is healthy but a trigger reverts to traumatic childhood and those ancient reactions.

Without a fence and a locked gate my fate was determined by accident or the irate.

A smart woman is an inconvenient woman who'd better have caution in dense generations.

There's no more respect for the little lady. There's only a hateful backlash from feminism see.

The minute they got an edge over me I was punished for all feminist-induced tragedies.

Triggering brings over-reacting but anger is healthy preventing us from hellish invading.

The invader had no self-awareness or parents just a grifter instantly creating hell and a mess.

ACTING LIKE THEY OWNED ME

In a social generation that wants to insult and bring you down a queen transcends the clowns.

I felt imposed on immediately. Swallowed up and about to be spat out--the social generation see.

Those boys have no respect for your boundaries in fact they hate them and will make you pay.

When I said I wasn't interested I was viciously attacked. Is there no more individual liberty I asked?

They hurt me so much with projections I only wanted the company of my pets or husband.

WITCH TYRANTS

Women can't lose fat cuz it's their only armor in a world that hates them, mostly other women.

You gotta conform to the B.S. of the female community, whatever it is currently.

And the women were CATTY. "Where'd she get all that money" they'd say of me viciously.

Despicable witches, go to hell. I stay away from your underhanded games you Jezebels.

What's worse is beta males who believe the despicable witches, sycophanous snitches.

That's the docile father afraid of mother or lawyer who sees you as bad from sister's slander.

I've been down that path of swimming upstream drowning yelling with no one hearing.

WOMEN ALWAYS ON THE HORN

Women were cheaply gossiping on horn all day playing out archetypes like Mafia Lady.

You had insiders and outsiders. The insiders got the jobs or the first or last bids on houses.

The women were viciously socially fascistic. Catty says it, die by a thousand cuts by asses.

Women are not to run the church but now they come to your house and bitch of course.

I hear people yelling at me and it's always women. When divorced from natural instincts, no fun.

As soon as I graciously gave em a RV hookup on the land they gossiped about me to everyone.

WITCH TYRANTS

Women don't have centuries of power sharing to know how to act. They always abuse it in fact.

Men stand for female power even more than women, out of terror they'll be found out by them.

If she's articulate with a brain like a steel trap he's likely to avoid talking but is then attacked.

Women are not to run the church but now they come to your home like an invading curse.

It's not a requirement for salvation that you go to any boring social potluck, remember that.

Unique male genius is allowed by men but punished in the female community based on conformity.

When feeling cramped and not admitting it to ourselves it ends in anger and blowing up.

All their sins were all-ok but they'd judge any type of new view/creative novelty as shady.

Smart women with high IQ don't want women to rule any more than men do. Harridans, whew!

The most sadistic camp guards were women. The men were bad but females can be vermin.

DUNNING-KRUGER EFFECT

Dunning-Kruger Effect is when the dumb have control over the elect cuz they don't get it.

They have the power though they're dumber. A helluva situation to. be in but I'm a survivor.

Dad said to hold my head up high lest this happen. Of being misunderstood and put-down.

WITCH TYRANTS

It's like they own your soul but only if you cave in for no one should control identity you know.

To be misjudged is hell but to play out their script like I did is degradation or death soon now.

They're mentally ill, they don't know what they're doing, forgive them Father, pray still.

Be patient with the mentally ill and treat them with respect if only to save your head.

JEZEBEL SPIRIT PREPARATION

Due to early rejection she clinged. Clingers are put through the ringer being thin-skinned.

In a sexualized generation most women have a Jezebel spirit so prepare/read up on it.

Jezebel is a borrower, a petty lifter, a home-wrecker and she's after your husband for sure.

Jezebel has pathological envy of everything you have with a flying monkey army on her behalf.

When she comes with her army don't let em in. She's primed em against you already friend.

LITTLE MINDS

The little minds will respond to the smart with hostility given a chance so keep your distance.

Maintain aristocratic reserve when around little minds cuz any involvement could turn unkind.

It eases resentment to realize friends warned you against em but you were still sick then.

WITCH TYRANTS

Someone with porous boundaries will soon realize their importance in hard lessons, aye.

Little minds will react to nonconforming females with hostility so try to keep things friendly.

They will form evil conclusions with no evidence if false accusation from the social is present.

Inconvenient females were taken to concentration camps by simple dossiers of neighbors.

The young white male bullies receded with the Mexican invasion and they were jailed/jaded/aged.

HEINOUS HIPPIES

They had children all over the place but never married. They were druggie losers with no teeth.

Don't resent past abusers without recalling friends' dissuasions against those losers first.

White boys weren't so hot anymore and didn't act as tho' they owned you, applying pressure.

Feminism and new demography slapped em down see, they ended meth addicts on the streets.

Instead of being pissed off at Sally, recall how everyone warned you about her dummy.

This was YOU--your lack of boundaries and naiveté from not being hurt enough to change.

Instead of resenting Jimmy, recall how everyone was worried about your involvement silly.

THE SLUT IS CROOKED

WITCH TYRANTS

The slut is crooked: she makes wrong decisions being out of grace. She brings bad actors ok?

The surfer-looking blond white boys were so arrogant they took right over/aren't so big now.

If you lived on the main street without a fence they assumed they owned you I guess.

The lawyer persecuting her in the name of the false family was a illicit sexual sinner see.

Getting past all that--family collisions & collusions--is such a relief, behind a locked gate, set.

The family opinion leader misperceives, the others follow suit and its a scapegoat system too.

It'll never end so I suggest you relocate. Start fresh, reinvent yourself, change your fate.

YOUR ENEMY BELIEVED EM

God didn't just take out my persecutors He rubbed out anyone who even heeded their slanders.

These people love to hate and they don't wanna forgive making you comfortable again.

Ok you were crazy, your addiction kept you together for that era but you repented the error.

You repented. Now if the system can't forgive you, drop em. Go on to the future hon'

Yes, you had a demon in you who made you do absurd, ridiculous things, an obnoxious fink!

It's as common as dirt what you went thru. It's the Hero's Path: WAY Down then Up, Whew.

WITCH TYRANTS

I had to be imposed on by a gang of boys to learn the most important lesson of boundaries.

Stop feeling no one's as depraved as you. Anything happens with a demon, forget that too.

The Fallen Hero Syndrome is part of the journey. You keep your head high after that believe me.

The "nigredo" stage in making gold is: "no one's as bad as me". We all go through it see.

Their invasion was traumatic and my over-excitability [OE] added to that to morph or reinvent.

OBSTACLES ARE TRAINERS

I needed the invasion to achieve my highest equation with a boundary hedge like a mountain.

It was horrible. I had no idea kids were so anarchical but it's the result of education sexual.

The youth chum up instantly--the result of the social culture I abhor. You vet before you adore.

Those creepy socialized and sexualized kids are now meth addicts on the streets or lunatics.

The females have had so many sexual partners they're jaded by forty and usually very angry.

Before computers we were ruled by social dynamics but now I could happily go beyond it.

GENERATIONAL ENVY

Old crones try to crush younger women making them conform: cackling harridans all around.

WITCH TYRANTS

Mothers jealous of their own daughters, daughters-in-law problems, jealousy triangles and slurs.

Makes ya wanna die of embarrassment. We swam in muddy waters, didn't know any better.

One thing about repentance is the bad memories get more intense since you're alert to sins.

Once you realize God was watching the whole time you change your tune, divinely groomed.

To see a woman chase a man is disgusting, demeaning, embarrassing. So much has changed.

The bible says a man finds a wife, not a wife finds a husband! Men do chasin, we the prayin'

LET IT SINK IN: YOU NEED PROTECTION

Let it percolate, let it all sink in. Give it time: take a walk/lay in the sun, prepare for visitation.

I had no idea the trouble I was in until denial lifted years later in my room-- marriage or doom!

A woman seeking independence that much--exiled to the wilderness--was hated a bunch.

He's the prize and you're not, that's the message. Well I say to hell with that, you're precious.

Your moral persecutors are worse sinners themselves, we finally see this when denial lifts.

It was my snootiest most stiff-necked persecutors who were closet sinners I found out later.

After recovering from addiction some must relocate or suffer unforgiveness/persecution.

WITCH TYRANTS

God's justice is necessary for the RELIEF of the saints. But vengeance is MINE God says.

You were a diamond in the rough. What of those ruffing you up on the way up? God took em out.

If you take vengeance, God won't. He'll do it better I swear and seeing it brings growth.

Living in the disorder of a hoarder make you hate her but recall it's a mental illness of mother.

THE SPIRIT OF FAMILIARITY

A spirit of familiarity emerges: they expect you to keep giving, forgetting all you've done for em.

More given, more expected. The very first time the future preacher stole he was arrested.

If you've got goals you gotta be willing to say NO! to friends and family lest you fall below.

If they ask for [drug] money and your spirit is grieved you gotta say NO. It's what you know.

My spirit was grieved every time I talked to him. He busted my boundaries never learning.

The one effect of narcissists is you feel exhausted and depleted from being in their presence.

They're users: the sucking spirit prevails as they eye your environment for great steals.

Don't get such a big house requiring housekeepers who gossip about you and the mister.

All those troubles and embarrassing faux pas molded you in a certain way, perfectly adapted.

WITCH TYRANTS

The heart is darkened when God is abandoned then God abandons the darkened heart.

What God condemns they affirm. What God punishes they exalt. Shocking really, the dem party.

THE FALLEN PEOPLE/CHURCH

The church is a collection of former fornicators cuz we were all sinners even some preachers.

"So were some of you" implies it's not genetic but a choice. You were but now you're not.

They had the gospel cinched but allowed so many more things they're now bewitched.

They saw me in a bad light with nothing I could do cuz it's the Dunning-Kruger Effect.

Concentration survivors said they'd never trust humans again and it's the same with you friend.

I was entangled in sick system dynamics and was always nervous. Now behind a gate, joyous!

Your guest is a third nostril and like fish after three days she smells. Never again/stay well.

Were cops mean and persecutory or was God using them to prune you of errors suddenly?

THE EVERCHANGING NARCISSIST

The narcissist is endlessly mutable. He can slip thru a keyhole, he can be young tho' old.

I didn't make him alcoholic dear he resumed his drinking career after being a sober actor.

Don't let em in. Get over this "nice hostess" thing. That's your domain where angels remain.

CHILDISH SILENT TREATMENT

Silent treatment is a childish game immature men play. Adults talk it out or end things amicably.

The silent treatment by immature men is to train the woman to make her feel less than.

You're not gonna play games anymore. Be an adult and learn relationship skills or suffer.

Art and science discoveries come thru a person so studying to be a vessel that's the reason.

Don't make too much of yourself or you'll implode in a fallen hero syndrome or suddenly old.

You've had enough of his one-way conversations or hoping for a little interest now gone.

You've had enough of sad homesick feelings around an empty fella--put focus on SELF now.

EMPTINESS AND HOMESICKNESS

The very smart can end in a ditch by not knowing who and how they are, and standing by it.

It is the very smart who must have the highest boundaries or be crushed by the mob.

This is the era of SOCIAL not independence or uniqueness so be careful your highness.

I'm the opposite to a fame whore. Your vulnerability goes up sky high the more the exposure.

WITCH TYRANTS

Choose an image that won't wear out in parts when you could be filling out in wholes.

I know who and HOW I am: I like privacy, have high boundaries and feel imposed on easily.

A MAN FINDS A WIFE NOT REVERSED

Men may feel they're the prize and she should compete for them not the opposite.

It's the man finding woman/a good thing, not the woman finds the man, chasing him.

Men may see her as needy and available--easy--all cuz she's chasing men like crazy.

A man should exert all energy and do everything for that one woman not be chased by them.

The fast women are not respected by men. When too easy they don't even think about em.

Husbands appreciated an orderly house but now poor housekeeping is a reason for divorce.

Poor housekeeping: first comes rejection and loss then hoarding and walling people out.

Once they start to get rid of stuff the relief is so great it takes them the rest of the way/new day.

He was a cute but brash kid but with the years he became a craggy evil man for sure.

IMPERATIVE THINKING OF PRE-ADOLESCENTS

Imperative Thinking is pre-adolescence: You do this or that as I think and say and I accept you.

WITCH TYRANTS

As the years pass the evil is more entrenched. A cute kid becomes obdurate, a bloated couch.

In a social generation being a recluse can get you killed/they don't understand privacy still.

Being a novel thinker can get you killed in a brainwashed era so be careful/keep still.

Understand social hypnotism or social psychology and you'll see it as a herd acting predictably.

Being a novel thinker can get you killed in a brainwashed era even in freedom America.

They were so stuck in pre-adolescent imperative thinking they demanded I come with them.

I didn't even know them, had never met them--but they acted like they owned me immediately.

This was pre-adolescent thinking being ruled by evil children. It was surrealistic and frightening.

Being ruled by evil children marks the evil times described in the bible, and now I know.

NEEDY FEMALES

Needy females seek desperately for the key to his acceptance, in trying to fit the narcissist.

She molds herself to get his response. This is not a way to live and shouldn't be what you want.

He goes silent as a "no" answer and responds when she hits on the right thing for his "yes".

Adapting to ungodly men is no way to live and will only bring increasing degeneration and ruin.

WITCH TYRANTS

I never knew how to keep things stable cuz he'd easily fly off the handle, my nerves frazzled.

There is only one key to anyone's acceptance and that's self-awareness/developing talents.

Get into your own thing, the things you're good at. These are gifts and they bring rifts.

The world us ruled by young males who think pre-adolescently and it's a gang mentality.

LIVING IN GANGLAND HYPNOSIS

Your own sisters handed you over to the enemy many times but you were in denial, aye?

Living in this gangland social hypnotic world a woman man not have freedom until marriage.

Gang mentality, social mentality: people hanging together, no privacy allowed whatsoever.

They demanded I come with them, know nothing about me at all. It was so uncivil/Neanderthal.

These types take their psychological cue from "out there" in the environment but we don't.

Never fret cuz a sentence isn't carried out immediately. I waited 30 years after your crime spree.

HE'S THE HIGH PRIZE NOT YOU

You're tired with a narcissist who sucks out what he wants and leaves the rest/couldn't care less.

Suddenly you see you were nowhere near as important to him as he to you, but no one is Sue.

WITCH TYRANTS

The Message: He the prize, he high-value, you must meet his standards/be on his level.

Autoimmunity: Instead of attacking the poison person we attack ourselves and keep them on.

Is he someone you should want or would he be a rattlesnake in your cage? Think about it.

Looking back God even loved and defended me while still in sin--He knew me way back then.

THE HERO'S PATH IS ZIGZAG

The Hero's Path is zigzag. It contains a Waterloo but amazing success later too: fact.

It's not a vaccine its a depopulation device. You aren't being told they're dropping like flies.

In retrospect God was my Champion even back then when in sin, I sure didn't deserve it man.

When God saw me He only saw the finished product in the future--he saw thru my bummers.

Whatever, my detractors are dead, gone or senile. God defends His own better than Corleone.

And once I learned it all He put me in a mansion behind a locked gate: Vacation and ESCAPE!

It starts by putting up with things, then more things busting boundaries then going crazy.

God's wrath is not just natural disasters but also being suddenly surrounded by strangers.

It's not necessary to know what the trauma was specifically, just how pathology proceeded.

Traumatized, the corrective addiction becomes a blind spot/he can't hear you yelling at him.

Fake it all you want, unless God puts you up He can also pull the plug on your beauty: ugh!

Don't call it addiction, just a blind spot corrective action. There was trauma then reaction.

We are not to blame, it is not our fault. That's what the trauma survivor ends up thinking about.

Some will hate you for being pensive--in your head--cuz you're not attending to them instead.

The greatest marks of growing older is knowing how fast things can change/getting bolder.

You don't take wild chances anymore. You're no longer manipulated, cherishing stability more.

MY DETRACTORS/DEBATORS

He'd travel 100 miles to debate me every so often and I dreaded the waste of time so boring.

His detractors traveled hundred miles to debate Einstein too tho' he just wanted solitude.

"Superior" refers to character not color but we've been dog-trained to hate the word anyway.

We've been trained to hate the word "superior" like it's all the same, without calibration.

NARCISSISTIC OUTSOURCING

The thing about taking vengeance is God always does it better. Wait for it/He'll do it for sure.

WITCH TYRANTS

At the heart of the heartless narcissist is a black void, an empty hole he works hard to avoid.

He outsources his existence to deal with inner emptiness, it's all about other's acceptance.

The narcissist leverages everything around him to oursource/borrow another existence.

The phone rings, he feels great. It doesn't, he's lost and frantically tries to compensate.

Once he outsources he experiences it as his **OWN** trait and his **OWN** property: he's "got a Ph.D."

UGLIFICATION FROM SIN

He unwisely thinks he escaped the consequences of sin but he's lost all his creativity, borin'

Music triggers the mind to spin off to eternity, outa this place of the ephemeral and transitory.

He unwisely thought he escaped the consequences of sin but look at his unlovely face darlin'

No whoremonger stays handsome. He's got so many demons in him it's a haunted house man.

He borrows his existence from others then experiences it as his own trait, his **OWN** property.

He takes outer things and integrates them kaleidoscopically like it's all him totally.

Minds, places, circumstances are all integrated then he **IS** them--it's different from borrowing.

He **INTEGRATES** various things into his "hive mind"–patches of realities he's admired, aye.

This kaleidoscope is help together precariously via grandiosity and other cognitive biases.

This is his outsourcing. He does not realize what he's doing, he just FEELS SO ALIVE see.

The "hive mind" of the narcissist explains why he's so protean: totally different every time.

He's so elastic being that way. One time he's richly handsome, the next he's distorted/ugly.

He feels he exists but ONLY in his pathologic narcissistic space next to his supply.

He says he enjoys solitude but he's texting all day long. That's his supply lest he go ingrown.

HE'S NOTHING WITHOUT EM

The gist: If all external sources were taken away from him he would feel he doesn't exist.

Outsourcing: scanning for sources of existence and incorporating them into a collage of "I".

Solitary seclusion is torture for the other-driven without the tools to go inside to the divine.

The narcissist feels it's "him" like it's coming from inside but it's not, it's outsourced in time.

Outsourcing is the most common solution to the narcissist's empty, non-being problem.

He has many "existence agents" who define him but since it's all outer it's all a fake sense.

The country club, who he knows, his neighbors, his bloodline--it's all outer how he identifies.

Take away attention from narcissist and he crumbles to dust--gotta be a constant charge or bust.

A constant power charge of electricity is needed--for the empty it's the charge of fake being.

He scouts for existence agents then coerces, co-opts, collaborates, lovebombs or grooms em.

FAKERY BRINGS ASYMMETRY

And thus he feels alive from fake being, but instantly it creates imbalance and asymmetry.

Fakery breeds a feeling of inferiority and this is ego-distorting causing blatant inconsistency.

The narcissist is grandiose on the one hand but clinging and dependent on the other.

A narcissist is codependent for identity yet hates being so dependent or reliant on anybody.

To rely on existence agents makes him feel bad, inferior, injured, traumatized, mortified.

And so the narc is always one step from dysphoria despite recurrent ego-bursts fakin' ya.

Depressive reactions are the shame of being dependent, which he can never let go of.

Shame of dependency on abusing, withholding, frustrating, emotionally dead/absent parents.

Either patchwork outsourcing or substituting where he borrows in one swallow, introjecting it all.

"He sucks the life outa me, he's like a vampire" said friends of narcissists, the survivors.

WITCH TYRANTS

They suck your existence and become it, while your gradual disappearing is their rise to being.

They exist more & more the less you exist in a zero sum game: drunk husband wins over dame.

Christ brought a sword to divide us not to "bring us together". Don't trust the word "uniter".

YOU KNOW HIM BY NAME-DROPPING

To me a narcissist is known by social climbing, name-dropping and showy favoritisms.

At first I felt misery being friendless but God wanted me blocked from these influences.

God my Father wanted to work with me alone, putting thoughts in and seeing my reactions.

God wanted to work with me alone, that was the absolute highest thing I'd ever known.

Who cares if Patty and Lucy never calls, I'm with the Highest and Mightiest in the Universe.

After all, I am His creation, presdesigned before my birth should I choose the right direction.

They gave you nothing but trouble, why hanker over people just exist in your divine bubble.

LEARN WHO YOU ARE

God removes the STAIN of sin--extracting all the black in your history like it never happened.

The spirit will only strive so far with you. There comes a time when you're given over to the zoo.

WITCH TYRANTS

You may not be broke being a debauched bloke but it's a "poverty of ideation" or being yoked.

He was like a shining comet and superstar but then became dull, uncreative and lackluster.

Just cuz I respect you doesn't mean I'll accept your way and if you think about it that's ok.

You get a cold clammy homesick feeling around him--cuz he's empty inside while ingrown.

You're not in love with this one triggering butterflies and fear, it's the next one dear.

I'm a communicator but with you it's one-way or the highway and I can't exist that way.

Liberals love diversity and inclusion as long as their jobs and neighborhoods aren't ruined.

Not just no-contact but disconnecting emotionally so you can get on with a happy life sweetie.

The sweet little ladies are basically gone, they've died out. Feminists are so nice ya' know--NOT.

She thinks she shows how special he is by sleeping with him but he thinks she did all of em.

THE NARCISSISTIC INFLUENCE

The narcissistic influence blocks your ability to be YOU and that's the most important thing too.

I'm an endless spout. I don't always like it but have to do it cuz God puts something in all of us.

Chance favors a prepared mind so be ready. An event occurs & you're in the spotlight/money.

WITCH TYRANTS

It went away years ago, I saw it was a trauma bond with the bad mother archetype and WOW.

But I became an expert in Systems Theory and wrote >100 books on social psychology.

I was imprisoned by their evil projections as to what and who I was and I was defenseless.

Like a computer script I took their projections on and became what they said and mentally dead.

I had to literally escape and rebuild in the desert. On the Potter's wheel for many dry years.

Fused with the sick system, I became what they said. Separated, i found the True Self instead.

HUMAN FOIBLES DESCRIBED

I have fully described the foibles of human nature but don't forget we've got God the savior.

Have I therefore become your enemy because I tell you the truth? Galatians 4: 16

Bad mom archetype scared hell into me and along with two feminist older sisters I was unfree.

What I've learned throughout my life is that weakness invites the wolves then we've had it.

Don't conflate what you think personally with the cultural brainwash creating your reality.

What you think is NOT what you've come up with but what's been crammed down in classes.

God sees your final perfection not your sin so he punishes foes coming against you man.

WITCH TYRANTS

They don't get married and have children they come for yours to groom em: "You're lesbian".

When God is in something it's obvious it's all ok but if it grates/is irate it's no shame to WAIT.

It's the stupidest thing ever for her to have sex before marriage, giving ALL her power away.

You're just another slut cuz you didn't have guts to lay a boundary and stay there you nut.

The crooked lives and constant mistakes of sluts and whoremongers go on forever.

HIS HIGH CONTROL NEEDS

High control needs, self-absorbed and insensitive, low empathy, uncaring and superior always.

Don't abuse sex to block/hide from trauma. It's just like any other addiction turning against ya'.

Most have been traumatized, blocking noxious thoughts with food, sex, TV, alcohol, drugs.

Traumatized by cold apathetic mothers with divided loyalties, many with immoral activities.

Traumatized by feminist mothers who hate dad, support abortion and sexualized education.

And boy do they put down Dad. The consequences are so dire and on their self-image, so bad.

Feminists gossip constantly--that's how they fight. They're always on the horn inciting riot.

They are underhanded/contradictory and the kids sense it with frustration without apology.

WITCH TYRANTS

Not used to power, they make up rules as they go then switch when it suits them as things go.

The feminist mom imprints on daughter and son thru pure primal fear of a bottomless cavern.

Whatever she believes she believes wholeheartedly but changes with the herd's turning.

SHE GOSSIPS CONSTANTLY

They gossip constantly about their own kids and take counsel on the phone from witches.

But kids can't gossip about mom, that's a "family secret" they've had to guard all along.

Underlying bitterness rules but is veiled by "pseudo-mutuality and harmony"-- happy fakers.

Without an inner core of real power, she rules the kids by the advice of witches in gossip hour.

It's the blind leading the blind but since it's all confirmed by the media no one minds.

Her friends and associates determine the fate of her charges: THIS is female disempowerment.

She gossips at the spa, the bridge party, at lunch and wonders why her kids hate her a bunch.

DUMB WITCHES

The women don't know what they're talking about and many are communists: Lord come now!

She blabs so much she can't keep it all straight. Any zvengali can get the scoop to manipulate.

WITCH TYRANTS

Yak-yak-yak. Constantly calling and texting and NEVER going within, what a bore darling.

She blabs about all her business on the first date. This is so low class and men it aggravates.

The beta male may be lonely/odd and so select a mate who's very social to compensate.

She hooks him into social circles he'd be blocked from if alone. This is often the whole thing no?

So that's two things: modern women CHASE men and also have SEX with them: disgustin'

I didn't chase him, he asked me to a church function and to cook chili at the American Legion.

Whoremonger, slut--liberals don't like those words! But they'll go along with perverse behavior.

RULED BY FICKLE FEMINISTS

Who in hell would wanna be ruled by a fickle feminist? We've all had to adapt to the venomous.

Women were slim, sweet little ladies but now they're big, fat, masculine and many times angry!

But in a strange reversal which is very oedipal, the boy gets fat and is attracted to fat mates.

Though intimidated by his big fat masculine mom he still marries the same type of woman.

So obviously the sex instinct becomes perverted depending on the object, and it's dystopic.

And thusly we have explained Dysgenics--the degeneration of bloodlines into sick.

WITCH TYRANTS

PEOPLE ARE CRUEL

Even if he's not having affairs there's a general sense of phoniness he operates with I swear.

One person can ruin your life for decades. You're now a haunted house of demons not praise.

He don't want you but you're crazy about him. This is a soul tie of a queen who is broken.

Break that soul tie. You're not in love with "him" its the trauma bond he triggered by his rejection.

The early trauma triggers you chemically, emotionally, sexually and may feel like butterflies.

He triggers an early trauma bond making him king of your world you'd do anything for: a clown.

YOU DON'T NEED THIS

You don't need this dreary guy, he's horrible but unfortunately he plays you like a fiddle.

He don't want you but you're crazy about him. This is a soul tie of a queen who is broken.

With alcohol anything can happen while drunk--so put these memories ALL in a bag to go out.

A codependent is other-focused: they don't have a sense of self and it's sad and dangerous.

A sheep is asleep living out childhood programming. Suffice it to say we're all there at one time.

An actor in a play selecting mates and friends who mirror slots in our childhood: PATTERNS.

WITCH TYRANTS

The illusion is you're awake when you're not. An actor in a play which is repeatedly played out.

BREAKDOWN FROM PATTERNS

My breakdown led to my breakthrough as the outer shell was cracked and being removed.

When the illusion was shattered I discovered parts of myself I never knew existed or mattered.

These unique aspects would never have surfaced without these breakdowns/openings.

Breakdown + OE {Overexcitability] = explosive new identity and discovery never seen in history.

Sometimes you gotta eat humble pie for years but that brings the change thru self-awareness.

When everyone goes on his side [the social manipulator] that's when breakdowns arise.

The codependent thinks the problem is in him and he needs permission to feel anything.

Sick systems block individuation and success. Before then one is fused with others in a net.

Schizophrenia is being fused in a system without differentiation. Wellness is individuation.

SYSTEMS MAINTAIN HOMEOSTASIS

Systems maintain homeostasis. When she gets too high she gets an insult, too low a pep talk.

Estranged from husband she was "desperate for human touch" but adultery finished her off.

49

WITCH TYRANTS

"Desperate" for touch indicates an early trauma bond leading to adultery and it's not real love.

Human touch, intimacy, connection: when this desire becomes desperate it's a trauma bond.

When the narcissist cheats she will only blame those revealing who she is/her adulteries see.

Too traumatized to see herself: thru depersonalization one is separated, a spectator that's all.

FAMILY RELIGIONS ARE FALSE

Familial religions are false: Jesus came with a sword NOT to unite members high with low.

Jesus: our worst enemies are in our house. His sword divided mothers from daughters et. al.

With age you're ignored. If other-directed this is bad lest you wake you up to the Lord.

Let me think. You're a mental hazard. I need office hours/never come without calling first.

Much remorse is healthy fear of the dark side which you NOW know is hell to be eschewed.

You recall the burning caldrons of the dark side. That's not PTSD just God reminding you, aye.

Your therapy is this: They don't want you. Now make plans with the Lord your tower/Highness.

Your therapy is this: They don't want you. Now make plans with the Lord your Highness.

As you get older they want you less and less so you're just blessed to be with God I guess.

WITCH TYRANTS

Don't back into old age, always looking back with remorse. Look FORWARD, see the Lord!

Since they're gonna abandon you anyway, give up on em now. Don't hang on and you'll grow.

Grow up by seeing truth that hurts so much. Don't avoid this psychic opening with a crutch.

Don't look back, they don't give a heck! One failed relationship after another to FORGET!

POETS HIT HARDEST

A singer sings, a painter paints, a trumpeter trumpets but the poetess hits the hardest.

All those around you are holding you down: it means no-growth, bad decisions, addictions.

Tho' he appears to compromise, concede or consider you it's ALL a manipulative ploy too.

Old age is a releasor of structure--appearing as cosmic, infantilized, psychotic/it's all good.

A narcissist wants his mold and if you fit, good. He's not self-aware--that's for sure, heart of wood.

Old age is a releasor of structure appearing as cosmic, infantilized, psychotic or whatever.

You've gotta fit HIS mold and if you can't, just go. His control deprives him of depth, the gold.

If it's all about control he can never know you deeply, the rich fields of love, meaning, beauty.

He could never get into your depths, interests and talents in fact they're annoying nuisances.

He doesn't wanna hear of your achievements he wants to go way, WAY back to your sad past.

He's not interested in doing any work for self-awareness. Him knowing it all should suffice.

Relationship depth--where the fun is, the growth--is elusive to the narcissist, a sad thing no?

HE HAS NO INNER CORE

He has no inner core or real identity. He re-invents himself with tragedy, a master actor see.

He sees someone he wants to be and becomes that with a brand new matrix around that see.

The narcissist hates your boundaries, anything that restricts him from getting his supply.

It's all about what you can do for him, how you can help him along in his worldly aspirin'.

Stop needing approval from others because this all goes away as the years pass, no jest.

Better start your cosmic journey now, getting used to the higher elements: angels, God's love.

Cuz no one gives a dam, really, and when you leave this world all bonds dissolve into infinity.

If you can hop on his train he's glad to have you along. But forget it if you've got your own.

DOMINANCE NEEDS RESTRICTS HIM

Needing dominance cuts him off from transcendence where fun, happiness and magic is.

WITCH TYRANTS

If you get all riled up chemically it's likely a trauma bond triggered thinking you love he.

It's a soul tie if you're triggered chemically and sexually, it goes together dangerously.

They are BOUND by their dominance and can't think beyond themselves--a prison of self.

If you sense favoritism it is no good since God hates false weights and stiff-necked mates.

He won't talk to you but he'll talk to others--it's hell, you got your answer, listen to the inner.

DOMINANCE INHIBITS CONTENTMENT

Dominance inhibits true and lasting contentment--benefits only of higher qualities amen.

They can never have the joy of just raw unselfish service to other people/never their goal.

They can never have the joy of raw unselfish service to other people, that's never their goal.

Dominance inhibits true and lasting contentment--benefits to only higher quality men.

Being dominant they can never love purely. I'll love you if, always strings attached, touchy.

What can you do for me? Ok now we have love--that's exactly how they think, the narcissist bums.

They laugh AT you at your expense but will never laugh with you, dominance needs preclude.

Dominance means he can't listen to your heart and the joy coming from that from the start.

WITCH TYRANTS

The narcissist makes up his history to suit his needs. It gets embarrassing til no one believes.

They don't appreciate rich rewards from developing character, they don't need that sir.

I'm choosing freedom over your efforts to confine me to your warped and limited kingdom.

TO RELATE, LEARN OF YOURSELF

Only by learning about myself [e.g. privacy needs] could I know how bad he was for me.

They wanna jump into bed without doing the WORK of getting to know ya, they skip that part.

Going to bed with a stranger? That's outrageous but happens on first dates that are bummers.

Only by understanding things about myself could I see how he fell short, tho' I was entranced.

How he fell short: not giving a dam about me, making me feel abandoned/unwanted/unfree.

Don't go for this kinda guy and understand soul ties: He triggers a rejection bond/butterflies.

He may not coerce you thru violence but thru subtle put downs and female comparisons.

You're a mental hazard with your yapper. I just wanna THINK not track things that don't matter.

America is the greatest but not with the youth who hate us, taught by the dems and feminists.

Is there anything more sickening than a narcissist bloke sending pictures of himself out?

WITCH TYRANTS

There's a strain of women-hate never seen in patriarchy when respected as the weaker sex.

Biggest reason to move on: a narcissist kills your spirit. You're no good is the impression you get.

Killing your spirit means you end up feeling like a shell of a person as long as he's in the situation.

Low self-value is such a persistent ingredient you suddenly break away to again retrieve it.

Are you a victim of haranguing communication--a high level of disdain and superiority son?

It's an attitude of disgust or contempt: "You are so beneath me" is the message sent.

DIVIDED LOYALTIES

Divided loyalties is a big reason to move on. The other attachments are more important son.

Divided loyalties break into relationships and ruin em but with narcissists it's the whole program.

A narcissist doesn't even know who he is so how can he be true to you in your brokenness?

Your relationships are only as healthy as the secrets allow you to be. Dr. Les Carter

The narcissist may have hidden uses for money, didn't pay taxes properly or acted illegally.

Secrets, shifting alliances and identity reinventions make relationships bad with narcissists.

They're not accountable time wise, resent you knowing their doings, hide phones/whisperings.

WITCH TYRANTS

The air of secretiveness is there, it's pervasive and it's ongoing. I was broken from not knowing.

An imbalance of power & control means move on! A leader's influence should be from love hon'

A good relationship is mutual hearing but the narcissist says "I'm not hearing I'm TELLING."

Communication is one-way, coupled with low empathy and "why would I need to hear this" ok.

As a youth I didn't have the right tools to deal with stress from fools but now I do, whew.

How to deal with stress from fools: simply avoid them, block, turn your ship around, eschew.

HE DOESN'T GIVE A DAM, GET THAT MA'AM.

Since he doesn't care how you're deep or what you think, listening is held in low regard see.

A narcissist has a tight wall of defense and often stonewall: block you out/silently sulk.

A stubborn withdrawal which typically has a sense of punishment to it, that's the narcissist.

It's always abusive in various forms. Physical is most extreme but others cause psychic harm.

If you tell him he's hurting you he couldn't care less if it's true and never thinks of that too.

Dignity, respect, civility--remember these please! Now compare to his power devices that sting.

This isn't my ride or how I ace. I'm going to make decisions taking me to a better place.

What is the solution after learning all this? One thing only: You need to practice self-care.

Godly minds create Renaissance of genius, beauty and hope but dense minds ruin it all.

Dense minds create war, disaster and ruin but clear minds create beauty so encouragin'.

You can't drag the bad past into the future and expect it to conform to God's Plan when you mature.

It was horrible. She was horrible, he was horrible, you were horrible. Ok now forget it.

YOU HAD TO LEARN WHAT PEOPLE ARE LIKE

You had to experience that to learn what people are like: the limitless evil of jerks or the dyke.

Most great successes had to go thru incredible messes to build their battleship for wins.

It goes together: evolution of character and knowing how to handle/what to expect from people.

Thank God for the lessons bringing me to here--tho' they hurt I see the larger picture.

Life is in two stages: the preparatory stage and the success stage of genius and wholeness.

OVERCOMING NARCISSISM EVERYWHERE

Recall the narcissist is a sadist who WANTS to hurt you and LOVES it when you're sad, think about that.

Don't go there--don't take a chance of narcissistic rage coming out on you. You should expect it too.

ONLINE OBSESSIONS: STOP GOING THERE OUTA CURIOSITY OR BE PUNCHED IN THE FACE AGAIN MISSY.

WITCH TYRANTS

The fact is I've gone beyond you now. I find you very dangerous but I'm also bored--be gone.

I feel SO MUCH BETTER having gone beyond you now. You can't hurt me any more, I know the score.

BLOCK ALL CONNECTIONS
You can't get to me, I've blocked all connections and I feel so dam good, Lord be willing it continues!

For my OWN reality is happy, free, childlike, decent, colorful, filled with cuddly animals/NOT YOU.

The guff I took, the confusion and frustration. Then the blind elation, OMG I'm so glad/good riddance.

The boring details are irrelevant--I know the guff I took. The past is dead, the door is closed bud.

You made me so miserable I never knew what was up and just when it's good you erupted, good luck bud.

Maybe it's the culmination of so many prior relationships which were rocky, feeling treated like s--*.

But I'm free now, if that's the best you can do, wow. What a miserable old coot, one I don't wanna know.

MEANINGLESS DETAILS

Who the hell cares about all these details your propound as if they're important, yet they're NOT?

Once you know the score you gotta discard before they discard you--no hoovering back or be blue.

We don't have the nonverbal cues anymore, it's all virtual--so we take those signs very seriously, yes sir.

Remember: If you don't go back he doesn't exist and never did--you keep him alive to kill you dead.

CURIOSITY KILLED THE CAT

Curiosity indeed killed the cat. Don't let curiosity draw you back! Stay in the groove, just your map.

You gotta take better care of inner child for you're a self-partner. Don't let her get involved or lose her.

For this is not ATTRACTION but an early trauma and it's all about chemicals and it's very dangerous.

Anything triggering the early trauma of broken bonds evokes chemicals that feel good/addict em.

Don't bemoan past relational mistakes, it's about growth from a little bud to having what it takes.

Only one not busting my boundaries was my husband, even he lived in separate house on the property.

DEVALUATION HURTS LIKE HELL

You can't be stepped on, devalued, ignored or silenced all your life and not feel invaded even when safe.

I want to be alone for it's an inner journey to self and God, not conformity to others, they're all flawed.

You just have an inability to relate, or at least you didn't want to relate to me. Whatever, I'm free.

For there are now VIRTUAL manners to consider and I take em dam seriously sir, you're rude to me.

Man you hurt me so much I can't believe it. The treachery, the gossiping, the triangulating--I'm done with it.

WITCH TYRANTS

You hoovered me back through charm and I fell for it every time--great cause for alarm, God help me.

And to think how you built me up only to pop my balloon--sadistically enjoying my reactions like a goon.

How we treat babies, children and old people is who we are--and it's not looking good for us so far.

Black on white crime is ten times higher than the reverse, a trend we never saw fifty years ago of course.

HE KEEPS A NARC HAREM

You can be sure he has a narc harem of ready supply when you wear out/give up. Count on it.

He's a narcissist--that means he's EMPTY, going along with any flow for admiration and acceptance.

You can't be stepped on, devalued, ignored or silenced all your life and not feel invaded even when safe.

They disrespect you by their refusal to be courteous ok?You're ignored, they don't give you the time of day.

First you don't like them, then they work you up to like them, then they ghost you. Yuk, whatever!

Ghosting to one-up you, make you feel bad, cuz he's sadistic or just doesn't care--so forget him.

The narc is just playing a game or writing checks. This is the vernacular when dealing with narcissists.

A female genius has no friends. She can't trust women and she can't trust men--only God, amen.

Most of our culture is empty narcissism--this means we either find God or sink in our swill with em.

WITCH TYRANTS

If he ghosted you cuz he doesn't care, then fine--NEXT! If it's not that it's good character he lacks.

HE'LL INVENTS THE WRONG PLAN

He's gonna come up with the wrong plan--not God's for man. Something he contrived but so less-than.

I took em back to not hate em any longer--what a relief! But then it happened again with these thieves.

SIN: SWIMMING IN MUDDY WATERS

I swam in muddy waters, how'd I know they were a generation of ruffians and pit-vipers?

All great people had to overcome a war--it's the resistance-training we had to endure.

Sin becomes a viscous habit and literally a brain connection which keeps thickening.

Until the inveterate sinner becomes a walking robot and everyone hates him or her.

SIN is a possession building up thru time like cancer and thus the devastation of a culture.

To become a writer about sin I had to experience it in both myself and bad associations.

When sin becomes culturally-condoned and even encouraged the end of culture is near.

After cultural sin comes tyranny and the end of all free thought and Renaissance creativity.

When in sin you'll be unrecognizable to your family since you're owned by our greatest enemy.

WITCH TYRANTS

Sin is not a one time deal it's a pattern which grows and reinforces itself in disease and ugly aging.

The sinner looks cute at twenty but see him at 60 and then tell me sin isn't our enemy.

The sinner can't compromise nor give since he grabs everything for himself and even fibs.

SUDDENLY

It can be a wonderful or terrible thing to fall into the hands of a living God, I'm awed.

He can crush you in His anger or lift you up to world fame and success--that's His character.

And it all happens SUDDENLY so either you'll be awed with delight or shamed/killed overnight.

SUDDENLY you'll be wealthy or broke, suddenly you'll be disgraced or made a famous face.

Women were the backbone of men, home and culture but not now that's all been forfeitured.

Looking back my most important achievement was a good marriage THEN I could work, protected.

It's not education at all but the politics of victimology: don't improve just find the enemy.

Taught to be professional agitators or community organizers not renaissance thinkers or inventors.

The devil knows whether you have your armor on or not, there are clear signs from your talk.

THE DARK CLOUD OF FEMINISM

WITCH TYRANTS

I started to self-realize in my twenties and my liberal feminist sister reacted with hostility.

I was coming from unfettered reality and she from the liberal feminist narrative of utter conformity.

No matter who it is they will begin to take over the household and very few are humble.

It's hard to tell a guest they can't have their people over but you must or get rid of em forever.

Since WWII it's been all about the SOCIAL and thus our national IQ increasingly falls far below.

Are you smarter hanging out with people? You're better off alone looking out the window.

In solitude I enter a phantasmagoria but in the social I just wanna go home, to hell with ya.

FURIOUS FEMINISTS

She started her liberal feminist crap up before I had the tools to resist it, then deep depression hit.

What families have endured for 50 years with furious feminists encouraged by their liberal peers!

Encouraged by media and friends the furious feminist ruined her family/home by hating men.

They think they've a right to be furious cuz it seems so true they're being oppressed and killed.

In truth they have it so good it isn't funny--freedom being more important than the money.

Leaks from past and environment: like husband linking with liberals after saying he hated em.

WITCH TYRANTS

The liberal-conservative split in couples is deadly and pivotal and there's no bridging the gap y'all.

Because we live in two parallel news universes we hate each others guts and its getting serious.

I don't let it get me down anymore, I can't. I know what I'm dealing with and drop the thought fast.

It's a matter of enjoying THIS day and letting nothing get in the way like traumas of yesterday.

The sick system can't just enjoy the day they gotta bring this up/that up until you give up.

We're enjoying the lovely day and our work so they get restless and start bugging us.

BAN HER FRIENDS FROM THE HOUSE

Men: save your home by banning her feminist friends or risk losing your family/home, amen.

Her feminist friends are dangerous cuz women conform to others so ban em or be tortured.

Since they're friends she's talkin' about you to em and they're responding back with venim.

You can't trust feminists for a minute cuz they're not in true reality just a made-up narrative.

Go to feminist parade--they won't discuss nor debate, they don't know why they're just irate

When in sin or bad associations you got the devil in ya' and people respond wanting to kill ya.

Children are arrows to protect you but women use their kids as gophers to do their dirty work.

WITCH TYRANTS

Monster brats use threats of violence to intimidate and control, so throw em out or die before old.

ONE threat of violence is all it should take to shake you up and throw out this monster fake.

He's a violent and dangerous person who should be in prison but you call him your adoring son.

MAKING PRE-CONVICTS

You made him a pre-convict by letting him manipulate you and never making things stick.

In this era of feminism, divorce is a feather in their cap--it's superior to kill babies and do that.

I'm learning to value the quiet, peace and privacy I have now before things hit and I lose it all.

Superior man is independent, totally. No matter when or where he lived he's himself, free.

Superior man does not take on the cultural mazeway of his era, he sees all clearly instead.

They don't know what they're talking about so they use too many words: loquacious bores.

They think they know something so try to explain it with logorrhea: a massive outpouring.

Can you take events/gatherings with you? No, they are a waste of time and make you blue.

Everyone's a therapist, a counselor or coach now. It's all been cheapened and they don't know.

Women are the worst. It's frightening to behold the results of deviating from nature's course.

WITCH TYRANTS

Women have become the worst and have society's protection as they do their dirty work.

THEY CAN'T STAND IT WHEN WE'RE HAPPY

You should have dusted off your hands and said "I know you not" but instead you still hung out.

They can't stand it when we're happy in true reality they gotta trigger fights and tragedy.

Men want sex and tranquility/women want security but wreck it for both when they're left lonely.

Because you stayed in the ring your self-esteem plunged and you accepted the obscene.

SICK CYCLES: Just when things are tranquil they gotta rattle the cage, make stuff up, create drills.

As a teen, getting drunk with mom was such a relief after years of being her victim deceived.

My only attempts to self-vindicate was to say: "I will write about you for the rest of my days".

Right after my words she died, finally knowing that I wasn't so dumb and it was her who lied.

When I started writing journals and organizing my disparate thoughts I found myself.

For my thoughts were hellish and terrified, how'd I know I could control what I despised?

How'd I know who I was and how'd I know who they were--chaotic, cruel, immoral and weird?

When weird and cruel is accepted as "cool" and they're socially-driven they naturally think they rule.

WITCH TYRANTS

BE MINDFUL TO BANISH PAST THOUGHTS

Most of the ground gained by Satan in our lives is from the open door of unforgiveness.

Mental illness is to be _profoundly well-adjusted_ to a profoundly sick society.

The mind is its own place. It can make a heaven out of hell or a hell out of heaven. John Milton

By continuously/upon awakening thinking of bad past I'm making a hell outa my heaven at last.

Thoughts are things and powerful things at that. Napoleon

All bad came from influences of substances or people-harassment but alone, it's a blast.

Their spirit would come right in: I had no boundaries and was easily controlled by my thin skin.

I would act out their thoughts or become what they said I was: this was my nightmarish past.

A Ph.D. isn't proof you've worked out your deepest issues or are likely to.

Unless "strength" is based on morality she makes a fool of herself saying she's strong, really.

Unless "good" is based on morality she makes a fool of herself saying she's good, embarrassingly.

THE END IS ALL THAT MATTERS

The biggest tragedies in a life create the most fantastic remedies in a higher path crystalized.

Had I not been mercilessly harassed, stalked, robbed and abused I wouldn't be a poetic recluse.

WITCH TYRANTS

Had I not been demeaned by hateful sisters I'd have never written books on the feminist disaster.

It all works together in the END: "ends well" is all that matters and we see the larger patterns.

I had to endure disaster to find the pearl in all matters and to write about it all to you seekers.

It hurt like hell but now whole and happy it's all ended VERY well cuz I spend time with God {under His spell}

You rattled their cage with envy before, all that stored bad energy will now target you for sure.

Liberals are insane--they can't accept the simple obvious truth: blue cities ARE shit-holes.

This is just the bluster of rear guard action. No worries we're winning and most of em are gone.

Liberals take truth as a great affront when it's as clear as the nose on their petulant mug.

LIBERALS HATE OBVIOUS TRUTH

Saying nice things about the wretched is more important than dividing good from bad.

It was not so in the old days of clearly dividing good from bad for blurred lines make us sad.

We give honor to the sinners now, we won't allow any criticism of their stinking habits: wow.

What is a shit-hole country? No plumbing, streets nor infrastructure and run by gangster money.

Seeing the obvious is now "racist" but forbidding clear perceptions creates mental illness.

WITCH TYRANTS

They're so outa touch it affects music preferences. Pat, mediocre, cantankerous, obnoxious.

I was **FREE** until she moved in then my reality became a thorny hurtful black cloud and tragedy.

I was **HAPPY** until he moved in then my entire life was about saving my shattered identity.

This identity struggle with my sisters was so intense it made me into a complete recluse, a mess.

What they were telling me I **WAS** was the opposite to the True Self and it was a house of horrors.

What they were telling me I **WAS** acted like a computer program in me to act like an ass.

THEY IMPOSED ON ME CONSTANTLY

God put me in a situation where I was imposed on constantly without any boundaries.

I learned about **PEOPLE** real quick from this experience and even the churches became officious.

If you don't have borders people will run roughshod over you, I barely escaped with my life, whew.

Coming from a sheltered conservative household I tried to play Miss Nice Hostess to my guests.

Scottish saying: "Guests are like fish, after three days they smell" and I learned this lesson well.

To **MATURE** for me meant saying "NO" without guilt and appointment-only or forget it.

What may seem obvious to most was not to me, little Miss Domesticated Nice Hostess.

WITCH TYRANTS

Saying "NO" brought guilt and the church ladies chimed that I should welcome to the hilt.

Your life isn't empty you're just hidden behind God's hand! What a joyful realization of heaven.

MILLENNIALS ARE SOCIAL CONFORMISTS

Millennials are social conformists who must timidly tow a line that keeps changing, what a mess.

When the clear man walks into a room he reads all their thoughts and it's an overwhelming knot.

Liberals will tell you what to think but also what you should be sad about or see as stink.

Superior man transcends time and parochial--he's the same across time and space ya' know.

It's one silly social event after another, as if gatherings are the only thing they need for survival.

Attachment traumas: Because he was wrong the split hooked you for years until you saw about him.

ATTACHMENT TRAUMAS

Man is fallen and in his fallen nature he will naturally sin and do crazy, illogical and devilish things.

The things I said and did as a fallen being were insane so I don't go back as God erased them.

Bad associations also act as a trigger for irrational autonomisms {uncontrolled bad behavior}.

Don't go where angels fear to tread: means don't put yourself in positions to be controlled/mis-led.

WITCH TYRANTS

They all think it's THEIR thoughts but really it's all implants--a 100-year plan not by chance.

Nationalism is now the default setting, the war is won-- but what we went thru invaded by scum!

The most insidious invasion was the globalist liberal MEDIA bringing our great country down.

CNN types: traitors paid millions to advance globalism and put down Trump/nationalism.

CNN types wanna create war so they can take over and destroy everything that we hold dear.

When you do not give them what they want they will destroy you because they are merciless.

OPEN BORDERS IS OPEN VALUES

Open borders means open values and that's a helluva fall for us Americans, the decent few.

Trump has outfoxed the elites at every turn. It's that type of savvy for which we should yearn.

Standards and ethics have slipped so much in the home that it's rare a kid comes out strong.

Liberals are so much about being "nicer" they are good to criminals, ex-cons and invaders.

In my forties I had a psychic opening about what I was to be: like the fifties, a sweet little lady.

Not an angry harridan like my liberal sisters saying they had a right to be ever/always furious.

To actually wanna help a man to become, even if it means feeding then leaving him alone.

WITCH TYRANTS

Not competing with or saying we're all the same--that's a myth which is entirely lame.

The kids are so warped they don't know how to act in your house--they are mal-adapted and scarred.

If they've been beaten up they'll beat you up, violence is WAY WAY up, so please watch out.

I tried to help kids and all they did was overtake me, destroy my home and ruin my family.

LIBERALS ARE GLOBALISTS

Liberals are globalists. They want open borders, high taxes and tyranny by bureaucrats.

Biden-Harris Cabal: destroy military with wokeness, weaken cops and strengthen criminals.

They see our naiveté as a green light to rape the hell out of us. It's happening, a ruined U.S.

The bad guys have hijacked our nation and they're wearing uniforms in very high stations.

These crazy woke generals are actually globalist agents to destroy the country fast.

The term "white supremacist" means anyone who loves America and common sense.

The end result of U.N. [evil globallist] supervision is we're gonna be paying reparations.

ERA OF DEGRADATION: HOLINESS IS SEPARATION

In an era of degradation the only holiness is separation as churches decline across the nation.

WITCH TYRANTS

If compromising churches are no different from culture what's the use--going is abusive.

Solitude is the only solution: unhooking from the compulsion to conform to deviation.

They've conformed so much to mediocrity I don't know they'll ever have attention to detail or finery.

God doesn't want you to ruminate over past faux pas, embarrassment, failures--just get clear.

The death of God's son--God Himself--was enough to erase these sins to be the magic elf.

So stop wasting time/procrastinating by thinking about Mary or Freddie and just GET READY.

These are the words the Lord gave me today to say. I've done that, so now enjoy your day.

INVASION THROUGH NEPOTISM AND PERSECUTION

They call for extreme intolerance of our customs/ways and extreme tolerance for ethnic/aliens, ok?

It's a Marxist-inspired tolerance that calls for putting down the citizens/putting up the aliens.

It's an inside-job invasion: the Marxist Tolerance of putting us down and them up in deception.

Instead of an army marching in they do it through nepotism and persecution: the Plan.

Just as almighty God puts one up while putting another down, so too are political decisions drawn.

If an alien comes into the family the liberal mother will fawn over him while you get a yawn.

WITCH TYRANTS

REVERSE RACISM IS REAL

The liberal dumb man will pay an alien twice what it's worth and the white man nothing of course.

The liberal woman will absorb an alien into the family while abandoning white sister for privilege.

All the dems have is racism and Russia which has imploded and racism is getting old with ya.

Making the dems defend Baltimore and the huckster Sharpton, what a brilliant move by our Man.

Genius Strategy: making the most radical & failed politicians the new faces of the democratic party.

We've won, no worries, we've won--but we're facing rear-guard action based on desperation.

The creative spirit comes thru two avenues: learned skills and total certitude through YOU.

Wives: Not saying anything is like a siren setting him off but pestering leads to sluggishness.

THE WHITE PRIVILEGE SCAM

They accuse whites of having privilege only to justify privileging the interloping minorities.

Cultural Marxists deliberately discriminate between the dominant culture and the left.

They intentionally privilege the minority cultures so as to destroy the dominant: TRAITORS.

They put the brown kids in mansions and us whites in shacks: that's the Marxist Tolerance Nation.

WITCH TYRANTS

They promote equality only to render the dominant culture as being unequal, inferior.

Cultural Marxists hate our nation and want only to destroy it--many times they have said this.

Our brilliant Trump has cast democrats as the party of The Squad and Rat-Infested Cities.

He's making Elijah Cummings and Ilhan Omar the FACES of the democrats: genius move by a star.

They can't say they aren't a rat-infested city so of course they race to the racism ditty.

Liberal logical fallacies: Attacking the man rather than the argument but we're used to this.

Ha ha. Again, the democrats are in the position of defending their own political disasters.

When I suddenly saw what was happening and what had happened I couldn't believe it man.

Wall will never be torn down as a symbol of oppression but of nationalism/globalist limits.

WALLS ARE NO SYMBOL OF OPPRESSION

Wall will never be torn down as a symbol of oppression but of nationalism and globalist limits.

The wall says: globalism doesn't define us anymore but nationalism, populism, traditionalism.

Populism and traditionalism requires BORDERS of course and this should be obvious.

Open borders means open values so cut that off (or we're lost) and the left loses it's voters too.

WITCH TYRANTS

Political paradigm shifts: when marginalized peripheral parties become accepted and central.

The churches: captured leftist cesspits?

People don't want children they want victim status--it's the new club of liberal fascism.

I'm not going to apologize for what Hitler or Ghengis Khan did, only what I did, but that's it.

If you accept the teaching of Christ and free market ideas it works like magic as God's plan.
Christian societies are the most effective and the wealthiest.

The rulers of this world are failures who chose the devil not God like the phonies in a church.

Stop cringing from bad memories or people and think of how God saved you from these evils.

ITS DUE TO IMMORALITY, NOT RACISM

They're immoral, rowdy, out of control kids so why do you say their failure's due to "racism"?

It appears Antifa is the muscle of the meth head left and war could be created fast.

If you got rats, trash and drugs what do you call it but infested, what do ya call it but disgusting.

If you got rats, trash and drugs what do you call it but infested, what do ya call it but disgusting.

Rats and feces all over but it's racist to say it? Cold hard facts vs. this is how they silence us.

When 12% of the country commits 50% of the murders, it's not racist to say it.

WITCH TYRANTS

As Christians we're supposed to be different, but God warns we'll be rejected because of it.

CHRISTIANS CAN'T CONFORM

As soon as we come to Christ the tendency to conform to their norm dissolves and is gone.

Come to Christ and you won't know how to conform you're just different but mean no harm.

We don't realize how we're influenced by the Spirit of God until it is removed from the flawed.

I took Him for granted and when the Spirit ceased striving with me it was a horrible tragedy.

Deep sin spiraling down to hell: Shock of all shocks but pray to Jesus and He'll get you off.

Once you're on Satan's train you become the caboose and all forces bring you down again.

Sin keeps you longer that you thought, costing far more like you have holes in your bucket.

When in sin you're possessed, controlled by evil evinced by what you do and say to people

Complacent sinners don't realize they're still being influenced by God's Spirit on the earth.

WITHOUT GOD'S SPIRIT IT'S MAD MAX FROM HELL

Without God's spirit on the earth it would be hellish, a Mad Max scenario of chaos, RATS and trash.

Things changed in seventies and respect was lost for all authority/teaching college was humiliating.

WITCH TYRANTS

As a lecturer they threw paper airplanes at me for not saying "and she" whenever I said "he".

To no avail, I said "he" is a non-personal pronoun referring to all mankind male and female.

I was unable to handle the audience and this meant disaster and collapse of a career of talk.

Impossible to handle a bunch of jerks in the audience who wanna shut you down: I was gone.

I regrouped--all people removed--in the desert and found a talent for pithy oneliners, the terse.

When respect is lost how can you lecture to a petulant, narrative-driven and debauched audience?

The more spiritual you are the more warped you get with autonomisms--and you can't help it.

The more proficient you are the more accurately you reflect the devil when up to no good.

The more articulate you are the more you can slash, burn and torture with lifelong scars.

It's not that women are strong but that men have become weak. Jesse Lee Peterson

Sis wanted to institutionalize me for delusions of grandeur, until now no way to prove it to her.

Joseph loved God and had a dream--next thing he knew he was in prison and chains.

But everywhere Joseph went he ended up in charge, like in prison he became the head guard.

LIVING IN A GHOSTTOWN AND GETTING STRONG

WITCH TYRANTS

I regrouped--all people removed--in the desert and found a talent for pithy one-liners: terse truths.

Without God's spirit on the earth it would be hellish, a Mad Max scenario of chaos, rats and trash.

God wants you clear of past remorse so realizing it was just a demon clears the slate again.

If God's spirit is removed from the peculiar Christian the whole world rises up against him.

Living in a ghosttown alone made me so strong inside I could handle anything in my stride.

I built a high wall after being serially imposed on for years and every day is paradise/no tears.

I lived in a tiny cabin way way out BUT without a fence I was bothered at least once a month.

In learning to deal with constant impositions I built a battleship then my reward: a relocation.

BORDERS AND BOUNDARIES MEANS PARADISE

Borders, boundaries: necessary for paradise and continuance of OUR values as a community.

If someone's in your environment, gotta adapt to their personality--that's too much for you and me.

Don't let em in cuz it's CONTACT then CONQUEST. The mere contact makes a mess.

Can't just love God on the mountaintop you gotta make it thru the valleys and I did that.

I think emotional pain is far, far worse than physical pain--broken heart or headache?

I stayed under tremendous hardship and accepted it. I became happy in a cabin, decrepit.

When I had learned enough/been punished enough or whatever, God rewarded with new endeavors.

When the right moment came God wrenched me free from a tiny dusty cabin to a mansion.

Finish your goal tho' you experience adversity. It's not hard to start but to complete it, see?

NEW LEVEL NEW DEVIL: OPPORTUNITY MEANS ADVERSARIES

A wide door of opportunity open to me and along with it many adversaries. 1 Cor 16:9 Paul.

Half of the scriptures about suffering are about God delivering us from suffering.

All suffering comes from my sins or other people's sins even though many are Christians.

A true Christian suffers persecution but they'll accept a carnal Christian.

When you live a godly life it convicts others who will come against you for it.

It amazes me how many fake problems the left tends to find in the best country in the world.

Academia of Privilege: Not dealing with real issues but making up things to be concerned with.

Schools villainize capitalism bringing millions outa poverty but love socialism, a tragedy.

Don't talk about policy just make the whole thing about racism and turn it into a moral campaign.

When you're successful and blessed, people you want to be excited for you will be JEALOUS.

WITCH TYRANTS

Don't ever want what someone else has unless willing to do what they did to get it. Joyce Meyer

DOUBLE FOR YOUR TROUBLE

From now on let no man trouble me. I bear in me the marks of Jesus Christ. Paul

Whatever He takes he returns tenfold and puts us in the position for our Great Promotion.

Job was in a horrible mess but in the end he got back double everything he lost/was blessed.

The churches have fallen. They're the ones for open borders and bringing the migrants in unvetted.

When injustice is suffered the bible says God gives us double blessing for former troubles.

I know my life is better because of all I went through than if I hadn't of, plus I'm brand new.

All things work together for good—no matter what we have the great privilege of trusting God.

Not everything is good, but ALL things work together for good for those who love God.

Do not wail "Why God why?" but rather say "I trust You and know You're completing this on high".

Mainstream Europe is now adopting the "racist" stance of the far right: spend on citizens first.

It's immigration vs. social services and it's Europe's LEFT that is waking up to all this!

Europe's paradigm shift is an astonishing transformation--the LEFT wants em out?

WITCH TYRANTS

New politics emerging all over world: Don't lose your culture via immigration–that's the pearl.

White man good bye. We're about to be swallowed up–It's the 100 year Kalergi Plan nonstop.

A modern American med school has become so crazy they teach em men can have babies.

Comin' to your door soon but they don't care about covid-positive migrants surging through.

The Lord said: prepare for visitation!

THE NEW GOLDEN AGE IS UPON US

A new conservative age is rising, a new renaissance and a Golden Age we'll be loving.

Returning to nation, culture, tradition, custom, religion, land, language, ethnicity of the region.

Populations are asserting national sovereignty with borders closing: bye bye globalism it was awesome.

As people revive their local customs globalism dies and a new post-globalist age arises.

What Great Again is all about: dislodging from anti-cultural globalist processes/getting out.

Voting out and if possible arresting the anti-democratic secular aristocracy who are so nasty.

The pressure was so great from the conflict then I went to God and He INSTANTLY forgave me.

God restoreth my soul after it was murdered by a false narrative and ideology spread by y'all.

WITCH TYRANTS

It was a hard way but because of it God did things for me that He wouldn't have another way.

What God gave me as recompense was worlds better than anything received from a person.

It grieves me to see the number of people bowing down to people when it should be God.

Don't give up your chosen life just to make someone happy who in the end won't even care.

Is it cheating to view pornography or have sex with a robot? Of course it is you nut.

The one-eyed man is king in the land of the blind and that my friends is what is happening.

Throw em out before they kill the things you love: your dog or cat and then finally you.

THROW EM OUT BEFORE THEY KILL YOUR DOG

The ruffian is a bum and scum and you gotta get rid of him. Take it from me, I was his friend.

Tho' a handsome young lad when he abused me when I saw him 30 years later he was old and ugly.

Decency and morality still exist because God's laws are the same then, now and forever.

Throw em out before they kill the things you love: your dog or cat and then finally you by thugs.

Black people were decent/moral people. They went to church and led by a father who wasn't evil.

But now they've changed and don't care about these things. If in doubt look at the stats please.

WITCH TYRANTS

Black people used to know how to communicate honestly but now that's all changed.

Having a roundabout erratic conversation with a black man is like arguing with a woman. JLPeterson

Don't ever argue with a woman or a beta male because they both live off of arguments man.

As Christians we gotta get rid of the I'll-get-you-back stuff. God is our vindicator that's enough.

Once you're born again, just BE. When in a fallen state you're just being but uncontrollably evil.

OUR FUTURE HAS NO ROOM FOR OUR PAST

Our future has no room for our past. When mourning ends we find God's Plan B is best.

"How long will you mourn Saul? I rejected him, it's over"--have the same attitude about him/her.

Stop living in regret, the biggest power-drainer. Whether you did or didn't, it's a loser.

The great "I Am" means He's here, at this moment, today: He can change things in a moment, ok?

You cannot fix anyone who doesn't want to be fixed but you can ruin your life trying.

Never let em put a guilt trip on you because they're not doing what they should be doing.

God may be leading by closing that old door that may have caused you damage down the road.

Instead of being frustrated we just have to think: Our times are in his hands-- our SEASON.

WITCH TYRANTS

Instead of rejection, think: God's got a plan I don't know about and I'm just gonna trust Him.

The old life may be familiar but stale and there's no anointing on stuff God's done with, ok?

There's nothing worse than trying to keep doing something that there's no life in.

His mercy is new each morning. Every 24 hours we get a chance for a brand new beginning.

EVERY MORNING'S A BRAND NEW START

Every morning's a brand new start but the devil wants you to wake up with anger or remorse.

Do not earnestly remember former things nor consider things of old for behold, I do a NEW thing.

He was a sinner, a tax collector and a thief but Jesus saw in him something he could work with.

The world is filled with virtue-signaling females who think they know how to rule but end up stupid fools.

A virtue-signaling phony female ruler will always end up sounding like ALL the others.

You said "prejudice is an emotional commitment to ignorance" or is it how they ACT, sis?

Racism is treating people negatively OR positively based on color of their skin: colorism.

Bombshell lawsuits coming out against AOC--I'm relieved to see it wasn't just me.

Historically genius dies early from drugs or suicide cuz they're always called crazy by the snide.

WITCH TYRANTS

How does Einstein relate to Jung? The energy affinitizes and meets thru the archetypes.

How does Jung/Einstein relate to morality? With sin there's a compensation in the moment, really.

With sin, we compensate: and that compensation brings disrespect (you're seen as low-rate).

They may seem to be helping you on the way up but you're dead with one one slip-up or descent.

CLUTTER AND NOT-QUITE-CLEAN

The godly good woman establishes routines for the house and that's how they all progress.

They call the decision to not-houseclean a "preference" but in truth is just dense.

For a man's personality is reflected in his environment. When he's clear, it's clear and simple.

Personality-in-environment: When it's kept nice his personality is more enhanced, amen.

House clutter is sapping, depressing, nihilism-making, nauseating, chemically killing.

I hated the junkman. He ruined my view, my day, my sense of space and beauty in my land.

Unless "clean" means exquisite housekeeping it's "not quite clean" which is really creepy.

You gotta scrub, sort, put things away neatly and in an orderly fashion or you're a bad woman.

FIND THE KEY AND IT'S ECSTASY

WITCH TYRANTS

The symptoms are so strong and deep it's much too late to turn away, talk about ecstasy.

Weight gain: jiggling flesh, clothes don't fit, feel bloated, lopsided, slow and undecided.

A world famous model [most beautiful of all] said at parties she goes right to cakes & rolls.

Yes man is omnivorous but he is also oligiphagous: existing on FEWEST varieties like me.

Eat once, snake diet. Eat twice, it's stuck and I wanna die if it doesn't move down darnit.

To start Daily Fasting forget WHAT you eat just get in the 22-hour fast habit and eat enough.

As you daily fast your food selections will continuously upgrade naturally/just get into fasting.

I recalled self-recriminating events then God said: the fast will delete all that like an ink blot.

Fasting is a divine lobotomy cleansing and purifying bad memories. It's all fecal matter see.

FASTING IS KEY TO BLISS

Fasting is the thing of total bliss and joy so forget what you eat for now in that little two hour food window.

I'm starting to crave salads--hallelujah. They're a great noon pick me up and scrapers intestinal.

Since men die early most women are widows, our final hurdle overcome before going home.

Don't eat to try to get your energy back up, fast then go lie down for a few then sprout up.

WITCH TYRANTS

Every time I take the day off it's a day I never worked so hard. Creativity evoked in leisure.

I'm an endless spout in continuous revelation but it's only in repentance that this happened.

Would-be genius has an incapacity for leisure but genius knows insights are evoked there.

Creativity is evoked in leisure. To start your work take the day off and your hunch arrives there.

REVERSAL DIETING AND INTERMITTENT FASTING [IF]
Alternate low and high carb in one meal, daily fasting

Man being oligophagous can exist on fewest varieties:: fruit, leaves, cheese, nuts, fish.

I didn't like the mansions they're more mausoleums I prefer the feel of cozy country houses.

Cherries & grapes the ultimate fast food. Even cutting a daily salad I can barely handle dude.

Cherries for breakfast, raspberries for lunch. Piece of cheese if hungry later or fast for a hunch.

Digestion uses 80% of energy raising total load on the immune. Don't eat past morning/noon.

Any one diet builds up so we want Reversal Dieting between all of em. You know em all hon'

Some days just shrimp and salmon, some days toast with cinnamon but fasting long periods with all of em.

Keto snacks filled with too many ingredients I don't want—a spoonful of almond butter is better.

They take adrenachrome then send pictures out. They eat animal then send pictures/YUK.

WITCH TYRANTS

Many Christians lately are putting down bacon--a leak from what they hear from Islam?

Are you: taking on the views of another religion not your own, putting down the bacon?

AIP: Reset immune system, prevent immune response, reduce symptoms of autoimmune disease.

It's not what I want to eat anymore, it's what is safe to eat without autoimmune reactions galore.

For money he killed his mother by not insisting she be revived when she coulda been viable to live.

The honey, fruit and pepperoni slice diet: Simply easy and autoimmune protocol-compliant.

Nothing's as profitable as studying all you need to know then just looking out the window.

He never cooked, existed on three pastries a day for breakfast and lived to be a hundred.

AUTOIMMUNE AFTERTHOUGHTS

I forgot all about the bacon. We eat cherries, grapes and melons.

Bacon grease restored the skin system after vegan devastation and I can't believe it man.

My Obama cut: 1/8" clipper once a week. So easy and my husband brags about it: sleek!

I'm done with the bacon just eating a few grapes or melons but pork fat works on the skin.

We may eat bacon but not again for months and just subsist on grapes, that's how it is.

WITCH TYRANTS

We craved shrimp so lived on it for a month then never had it again, that's how it is friend.

For man is omnivorous so don't let anyone peg you on diet or ridicule you for reversing it.

Ray craved beef jerky so I got a bunch in and he ate it for a week and never had it again.

I'm fruitarian by default whether I like it or not, just juicy fruits and butters of the nut.

Honey is an easy meal but maple syrup is better--spoon theory is how we end up later.

It works for satiety with no reaction: honey almond butter/white chocolate macadamia bars.

How to rejuvenate dry skin after veganism: Apply animal fats topically for instant results.

Need to apply vitamin-rich animal fats topically since our skin is the last to receive nutrients.

With an ulcer, hunger feels like nausea so after a while fasting the pain oughta be out of ya.

When you have an ulcer it's obvious food is the problem and it's easier to be fastin'

You get to a point where your health depends on how little you eat then energy's released.

It's the FASTING no matter what you're eating. Even a one day fast after donuts can be healing.

THE BACON BAROMETER OR LITMUS TEST

People have been Islamized regarding food. Even if a Christian they're afraid of the bacon.

WITCH TYRANTS

Since the skin is the last to receive, just one day without fat and it suffers unrelieved.

Wrinkles and lines form as nighttime evaporation of our skin and applying animal fat restores this.

Ok we had our bacon now we're all ok until our melon.

DON'T TOLERATE BULLIES

The most important rules of foreign policy are: don't be a bully and don't tolerate bullies.

70 million abortions: God's pulling outa the world now. He promised it cuz He's Justice ya know.

Don't kid yourself they gotta bullet for each one of us--the lovers of Trump and true patriots.

Bohemian Grove is an elite men's retreat with evil overtones worse than skull and bones.

Democrats tend to move to conservative areas then bring their blue policies with them.

Arizona will not let Biden abuse his authority, refuse to upload laws or take our sovereignty. AC

Got addicted to productive coughing thinking I was accomplishing 'til God said: just stop smoking.

The way to extinguish past thoughts is concentrate on your breath bringing you to the present.

Cycles: I walked over to where my worst enemy had moved from--and met my future husband.

It's insulting to God that we run to everyone else but never have time for Him, amen.

WITCH TYRANTS

I have to spend time with God each morning to get His daily training to create from nothing.

The characteristic of successful people is they don't let their past kill their future with evil.

Enough with the rehashed news no matter HOW important it is or commentaries too.

Rehashed news of just this ONE day over and over. Makes no sense—be a headline reader.

BE THAT CONSTANT SPOUT

I'm a prolific writer. It flows 16 hours a day but only after writing a thousand drafts four decades before.

I never have to force myself to write, only to stop writing and then move into leisure.

Been writing since midnight and now it's 7:am—I'm OFF for the day, goin' out on my land

After tortured by her tyranny she handed me over to a liberal feminist fiduciary, Lord help me.

Oh to become proficient in your niche after a lifetime of overcoming obstacles and the witch.

All that matters is work even if not here to enjoy the perks, with artists the work comes first.

I deserve it and you don't cuz while you were yakking & cruising I was working day/night/morning.

Dictators hate poets—they hit the hardest. This proves less is more like words of the Lord's.

They left sincere evangelism to run around the country, sign books, take selfies and pose.

Chance favors a prepared mind: an event happens and suddenly you're in the money/spotlight.

God chose me to be the vessel for this Creative Act and He also chose the link to success.

STATE YOUR FAITH IN SUCCESS

State your faith before you've got anything to show for it—when it hits they'll recall you predicted it.

You're outa grace doing that stuff and God'll put holes in your bucket while nothing works out.

God chose the TIME—an exact moment. He designed Creative Act and link before your birth son.

Why is FAME so frightening to some? Cuz they can't control it: the reactions nor the outcome.

It's a paradox an extreme introvert would be so bold as to state all that but that's the archetype.

More introverted = appears most extroverted in bold speech. It's ON or OFF like a geyser see.

Since we woke-up the globalist's only hope is to trigger a civil war which is labeled a RACE WAR.

Live in ETERNITY not this one day rehashed over and over, forgotten forever and ever.

So what if you can't get any attention from a lost generation with low tastes and minds.

It's not women I anti-male/family chip on shoulder support of police state we hate.

Corrupted by the system he joined, he lost his honor and then lusted for luxury and power.

WITCH TYRANTS

CAN'T FORCE SUCCESS, PREPARE & WAIT

Can't force success, it's unattainable that way, but continue to prepare your mind for that day.

When it comes to intel I want the best and brightest not the least whitest. Adam Carolla

With God it's all about TIMING. Things aren't willy-nilly they are EXACT—so are you ready?

God's pulling outa the world now and you're gonna be left with evil—forced to wake up people.

The old guard are dead so NO one remembers you in your primitive stage or fallen instead.

What is my purpose, to write nursery rhymes and verses? If so I'll do it of course sis.

I hate phoning cuz they go off at the mouth and it's boring. Just email: recorded and orderly.

Once they start to save stuff it perverts to also saving trash. Hoarding is truly a mental illness.

YOUR TIME HAS COME

This is your time, it's finally come. Grab onto it cuz there is only decline from here on.

My only escape is music—even short stories I can't track but instrumentals are galactic.

All's well that ends well, remember that. All that stuff you went thru was crap off your map.

You had your Waterloo—lasted decades too—but it all evens in the end, you're sweet/no shrew.

WITCH TYRANTS

Unresolved wounds make one toxic and also explains the mean culture evolving so quick.

It is important to remember they are mentally ill. Treat them with calm, patience and respect.

FRIGGIN' PHONES & HISTORY BUFFS

They always wanna talk on phone & get angry if you won't. Tangents, rants, voice cancellations.

The phone gives em a chance to blow your time or rant on something, just EMAIL ME darling.

They're so used to phones they're offended I won't use em--what'd they do before this invention?

You say something I say something then you say something...how boring I'd rather be writing.

Hitler saw no one cared about the Armenian genocide so it'd be the same with the Jews, aye.

He told them to turn away from false religious teachers who were leading them to hell.

Jews made Hitler's perfect scapegoat cuz no one would help em and he needed their money.

It's faceless radicals never known that are running the show: Whitehouse/DHS staff et. al.

The wife said to husband "please get off of me, it's not your birthday" and that's routine see.

Whatever video you're intently watching, there's a billion you're not watching--think of that.

Be as independent as you can but don't be reluctant to ask for help--it's a fine balance no?

"Keep right on to the end of
the road, that's my motto".
Last words by 102 year old.

The best talents ripen late.
What are those talents?
Those bringing people to God,
so wait.